Hope

Heaven's Own Gift

PAINTINGS BY

Sandy Lynam Clough

Christian Art Gifts

I wish for you faith ...
I send to you hope ...
I share with you love from a joyful heart.

—SANDY LYNAM CLOUGH

Hope – Heaven's Own Gift

Copyright © 2001 by Sandy Lynam Clough
Originally published by Harvest House Publishers, Eugene, Oregon 97402

This edition copyright © 2002 by Christian Art Gifts,
P. O. Box 1599, Vereeniging, 1930, South Africa. All rights reserved.

All works of art reproduced in this book are copyrighted by Sandy Lynam
Clough and may not be reproduced without the artist's permission. For more
information regarding art prints featured in this book, please contact:
Sandy Clough Studios, 25 Trail Road, Marietta, GA 30064
1.800.447.8409

Design and production by Garborg Design Works, Minneapolis, Minnesota

Harvest House Publishers has made every effort to trace the ownership of all
poems and quotes. In the event of a question arising from the use of a poem
or quote, we regret any error made and will be pleased to make the necessary
correction in future editions of this book.

Scripture quotations are taken from the Holy Bible, New International
Version®, Copyright © 1973, 1978, 1984 by the International Bible Society.
Used by permission of Zondervan Publishing House; and the New King
James Version, Copyright © 1979, 1980, 1982 by Thomas Nelson, Inc.,
Publishers. Used by permission.

Printed in Singapore

ISBN 1-86852-823-5

02 03 04 05 06 07 08 09 10 11 – 10 9 8 7 6 5 4 3 2 1

Every hope or dream
of the human mind will be
fulfilled if it is noble and of God.

OSWALD CHAMBERS

Hope is one of the greatest gifts we have been given by our heavenly Father. It carries no price tag but its value is priceless. We cling to it when the future looks uncertain and praise it when things turn out better than we could have ever imagined. Hope is the foundation on which we build our dreams and aspirations. It has been the cornerstone upon which ordinary people have accomplished extraordinary things.

Hope will always endure.

Hope

Sandy Lynam Clough

What oxygen is to the lungs,
such is hope to the meaning of life.

EMIL BRUNNER

Learn from yesterday,

live for today,

hope for tomorrow.

Anonymous

May the God of hope fill you with
all joy and peace as you trust in Him,
so that you may overflow with hope …

The Book of Romans

Hope is a state of mind, not of the world. Hope,
in this deep and powerful sense, is not the same as joy
that things are going well, or willingness to invest in
enterprises that are obviously heading for success, but
rather an ability to work for something because it is good.

VACLAV HAVEL

Hope is a risk that must be run.

GEORGES BERNANOS

Be joyful in hope, patient in affliction, faithful in prayer.

THE BOOK OF ROMANS

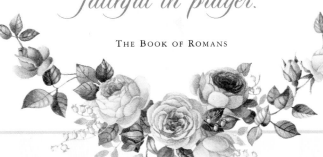

Man is, properly speaking, based upon hope,
he has no other possession but hope;
this world of his is emphatically the place of hope.

THOMAS CARLYLE

"Hope" is the thing with feathers —
That perches in the soul —
And sings the tune without the words —
And never stops — at all.

EMILY DICKINSON

Great hopes make great men.

THOMAS FULLER

9

Hope, like the gleaming taper's light,
Adorns and cheers our way;
And still, as darker grows the night,
Emits a brighter ray.

OLIVER GOLDSMITH

*He who has health,
has hope; and he who
has hope, has everything.*

PROVERB

And thus, oh Hope! Thy lovely form
In sorrow's gloomy night shall be
The sun that looks through cloud and storm
Upon a dark and moonless sea.

JOSEPH RODMAN DRAKE

Sandy Lynam Clough

It is difficult to say what is impossible,
for the dream of yesterday is the hope of today
and the reality of tomorrow.

ROBERT H. GODDARD

Never deprive someone of hope —

it may be all they have.

HENRY ADAMS

Be strong and take heart,
all you who hope in the LORD.

THE BOOK OF PSALMS

*Take short views,
hope for the best,
and trust in God.*

SYDNEY SMITH

Entertain great hopes.

ROBERT FROST

Hope is a gift we give ourselves,
and it remains when all else is gone.

NAOMI JUDD

Hope sees the invisible, feels the intangible
and achieves the impossible.

AUTHOR UNKNOWN

Such is hope, heaven's own gift to
struggling mortals, pervading,
like some subtle essence from the skies,
all things both good and bad.

CHARLES DICKENS

The capacity for hope is the most significant fact of life.
It provides human beings with a sense of
destination and the energy to get started.

NORMAN COUSINS

As long as we have hope, we have direction, the energy to move, and the map to move by. We have a hundred alternatives, a thousand paths and an infinity of dreams. Hopeful, we are halfway to where we want to go; hopeless, we are lost forever.

AUTHOR UNKNOWN

We live by admiration,
hope and love.

WILLIAM WORDSWORTH

We judge of man's
wisdom by his hope.

RALPH WALDO EMERSON

Optimism is the faith that leads to achievement.
Nothing can be done without hope and confidence.

HELEN KELLER

Hope is a strange invention —
A Patent of the Heart —
In unremitting action
Yet never wearing out.

EMILY DICKINSON

Hope is some extraordinary spiritual grace that
God gives us to control our fears, not to oust them.

VINCENT MCNABB

*The word which God
has written on the brow
of every man is Hope.*

VICTOR HUGO

Hope is like the sun, which,
as we walk toward it, casts a shadow
of our burdens behind us.

ANONYMOUS

And now these three remain:
faith, hope and love.

THE BOOK OF 1 CORINTHIANS

Hope is both the earliest and the most indispensable
virtue inherent in the state of being alive.
If life is to be sustained hope must remain,
even where confidence is wounded, trust impaired.

ERIK H. ERIKSON

Sandy Lynam Clough

23

Now faith is the substance of things hoped for,
the evidence of things not seen.

THE BOOK OF HEBREWS

Hope is the parent of faith.

CYRUS A. BARTOL

We must accept
finite disappointment,
but never lose infinite hope.

MARTIN LUTHER KING JR.

*Three grand
essentials to happiness
in this life are
something to do,
something to love,
and something
to hope for.*

JOSEPH ADDISON

A strong defense to guard the soul
Is ours from heaven above;
God fills our hearts with steadfast hope
And gives us faith and love.

DENNIS DEHANN

Men and women are limited not by the place of their birth, not by the color of their skin, but by the size of their hope.

JOHN JOHNSON

Each time a person stands
up for an ideal, or acts to improve the
lot of others, or strikes out against injustice,
he sends forth a tiny ripple of hope.

ROBERT FRANCIS KENNEDY

*Everything that is done
in the world is done by hope.*

MARTIN LUTHER

Hope is the pillar that holds up the world.
Hope is the dream of a waking man.

PLINY

Sandy Lynam Clough